NAVCLASSIC

Born to Reproduce

DAWSON TROTMAN

A NavPress resource published in alliance
with Tyndale House Publishers

NavPress is the publishing ministry of The Navigators, an international Christian organization and leader in personal spiritual development. NavPress is committed to helping people grow spiritually and enjoy lives of meaning and hope through personal and group resources that are biblically rooted, culturally relevant, and highly practical.

For more information, visit NavPress.com.

Born to Reproduce

Copyright © 2008 by The Navigators. All rights reserved.

A NavPress resource published in alliance with Tyndale House Publishers.

NAVPRESS and the NavPress logo are registered trademarks of NavPress, The Navigators, Colorado Springs, Colorado. *TYNDALE* is a registered trademark of Tyndale House Publishers. Absence of ® in connection with marks of NavPress or other parties does not indicate an absence of registration of those marks.

Cover design by Arvid Wallen
Cover image by Shutterstock

Scripture quotations are taken from the *Holy Bible*, King James Version.

For information about special discounts for bulk purchases, please contact Tyndale House Publishers at csresponse@tyndale.com, or call 1-800-323-9400.

ISBN 978-1-64158-011-3 (10 pack)

Printed in the United States of America

26 25 24 23 22 21 20
13 12 11 10   9   8   7

Editor's Note: *"Born to Reproduce" was originally a forty-seven-minute message, given to the staff of Back to the Bible in 1955, that burned deeply in Dawson Trotman's soul. It was later transcribed and published as a booklet that has been read by thousands over the past fifty years.*

In reintroducing this booklet to a new generation, our intent is to preserve the original language of this classic message. Scripture references in the King James Version, the use of male pronouns, and world-population figures reflect the original setting in which this booklet was written.

☙☙☙☙☙

DAWSON TROTMAN, converted at age twenty, gave thirty years to vigorous pursuit of the goal "to know Christ and make Him known." Trotman was a man who believed God, who asked Him for great things and saw God answer. The ministry of The Navigators, which Trotman founded in 1933, is one of those answers. He led the ministry until his death in 1956.

Foreword

In the summer of 1955 it was my privilege to meet Dawson Trotman, director of The Navigators, for the first time. My heart was thrilled not only with his vision of soul-winning but also with the manner in which God had used this man to promote a method of first winning an individual, then teaching him how to win and teach others, multiplying the ministry in this manner, supplementing the mass approach.

Through the years I have met Navigators who were trained by either Dawson Trotman or one of his men, and I have usually found them to be people with a passion for souls, a good knowledge of the Word, and something that made them stand out as individual Christians.

From the day when I met Dawson Trotman, our friendship and fellowship grew by leaps and bounds. We spent many hours together on various occasions, and almost overnight a David-Jonathan love grew.

As I came to know this man better, I soon discovered the secret of his power. Early in his Christian life he and another young man covenanted together to meet for prayer every morning for six weeks in order to find God's will in a certain matter. This spirit and practice of devotion was a rule of his life. He rose early to pray and read God's Word. Without this devotion to God he could not have been so successful in his service.

The unselfishness of Mr. Trotman could be seen on every hand. There was no trying on his part to hoard information or knowledge that he had gained in twenty-two years of experience, but rather there was a willingness to share and to cooperate with us in producing a much more thorough follow-up system for the Back to the Bible broadcast.

The Back to the Bible Broadcast Home Study Course, a follow-up method for young Christians, was the result. Different ones in the organization gave many hours of their time in helping to produce this course, and Mr. Trotman himself supervised every phase of it.

Possibly one of the last major accomplishments of this man was his untiring work in making this Bible course a reality. It was a pooling of both experience and knowledge, which we believe will bear much fruit.

Mr. Trotman went to be with the Lord June 18, 1956. In rescuing another person from drowning in Schroon Lake, New York, he lost his own life. How characteristic this was of his lifelong ministry! One man summed it up in these words: "I think Daws has personally touched more lives than anybody I have ever known."

The work of The Navigators continues under able leadership. It was solidly built on the principle of one person training another instead of one person being the teacher of all.

My own life is dedicated to a greater effort than ever before to persistently follow this great principle of Bible-memory work and person-to-person evangelism.

THEODORE H. EPP
Founding Director, Back to the Bible

A few years ago, while visiting Edinburgh, Scotland, I stood on High Street just down from the castle. As I stood there, I saw a father and a mother coming toward me pushing a baby carriage. They looked very happy, were well dressed and apparently very well-to-do. I tried to catch a glimpse of the baby as they passed and, seeing my interest, they stopped to let me look at the little pink-cheeked member of their family.

I watched them for a little while as they walked on and thought how beautiful it is that God permits a man to choose one woman who seems the most beautiful and lovely to him, and she chooses him out of all the men whom she has ever known. Then they separate themselves to one another, and God in His plan gives them the means of reproduction! It is a wonderful thing that a little child should be born into their family, having some of the father's characteristics and some of the mother's, some of his looks and some of hers. Each sees in that baby a reflection of the one whom he or she loves.

Seeing that little one made me feel homesick for my own children whom I dearly love and whose faces I had not seen for some time. As I continued to stand there I saw another baby carriage, or perambulator as they call it over there, coming in my direction. It was a secondhand affair and very wobbly. Obviously the father and mother were poor. Both were dressed poorly and plainly, but when I indicated my interest in seeing their baby, they stopped and with the same pride as the other parents let me view their little pink-cheeked, beautiful-eyed child.

I thought as these went on their way, "God gave this little baby, whose parents are poor, everything that He gave the other. It has five little fingers on each hand, a little mouth, and two eyes. Properly cared for, those little hands may someday be the hands of an artist or a musician."

Then this other thought came to me. "Isn't it wonderful that God did not select the wealthy and the educated and say, 'You can have children,' and to the poor and the uneducated say, 'You cannot.' Everyone on earth has that privilege."

The first order ever given to man was that he "be fruitful and multiply." In other words, he was to reproduce after his own kind. God did not tell Adam and Eve, our first parents, to be spiritual. They were already in His image. Sin had not yet come in. He just said, "Multiply. I want more just like you, more in My own image."

Of course, the image was marred. But Adam and Eve had children. They began to multiply. There came a time, however, when God had to destroy most of the flesh that had been born. He started over with eight people. The more than two billion people who are on earth today came from the eight who were in the ark because they were fruitful and multiplied.

Hindrances to Multiplying

Only a few things will ever keep human beings from multiplying themselves in the physical realm.

If a couple is not united, they will not reproduce. This is a truth which Christians need to grasp with reference to spiritual reproduction. When a person becomes a child of God, he should realize that he is to live in union with Jesus Christ if he is going to win others to the Savior.

Another factor that can hinder reproduction is disease or impairment to some part of the body that is needed for reproductive purposes. In the spiritual realm sin is the disease that can keep one from winning the lost.

One other thing that can keep people from having children is immaturity. God in His wisdom saw to it that little children cannot have babies. A little boy must first grow to sufficient maturity to be able to earn a living, and a little girl must be old enough to care for a baby.

Everyone should be born again. That is God's desire. God never intended that man should merely live and die — be a walking corpse to be laid in the ground. The vast majority of people know that there is something beyond the grave, and so each one who is born into God's family should seek others to be born again.

A person is born again when he receives Jesus Christ. "But as many as received him, to them gave he power to become the sons of God ... Which were born, not of blood, nor of the will of the flesh, nor of the will of man, but of God" (John 1:12-13). The new birth. It is God's plan that these new babes in Christ grow. All provision is made for their growth into maturity, and then they are to multiply — not only the rich or the educated, but all alike. Every person who is born into God's family is to multiply.

In the physical realm when your children have children, you become a grandparent. Your parents are then great-grandparents, and theirs are great-great-grandparents. And so it should be in the spiritual.

Spiritual Babes

Wherever you find a Christian who is not leading men and women to Christ, something is wrong. He may still be a babe. I do not mean that he does not know a lot of doctrine and is not well informed through hearing good preaching. I know many people who can argue the pre-, the post-, and the amillennial position and who know much about dispensations but who are still immature. Paul said of some such in Corinth, "And I, brethren, could not speak unto you as unto spiritual [or mature], but as unto carnal, even as unto babes in Christ" (1 Corinthians 3:1).

Because they were babes, they were immature, incapable of spiritual reproduction. In other words, they could not help other people to be born again. Paul continued, "I have fed you with milk, and not with meat: for hitherto ye were not able to bear it . . . ye are yet carnal [or babes]: for . . . there is among you envying, and strife, and divisions" (1 Corinthians 3:2-3). I know a lot of church members, Sunday school teachers, and members of the women's missionary society who will say to each other, "Have you heard about so and so?" and pass along some gossip. Such have done an abominable thing in the sight of God. How horrible it is when a Christian hears something and spreads the story! The Book says, "These six things doth the LORD hate: yea, seven are an abomination unto him . . . a lying tongue . . ." (Proverbs 6:16-17). Oh, the Christians I know, both men and women, who let lying come in!

"He that soweth discord among brethren" (Proverbs 6:19) is another. This is walking as a babe, and I believe that it is one of the basic reasons why some Christians do not have people born again into God's family through them. They are sick spiritually. There is something wrong. There is a spiritual disease in their lives. They are immature. There is not that union with Christ.

But when all things are right between you and the Lord, regardless of how much or how little you may know intellectually from the standpoint of the world, you can be a spiritual parent. And that, incidentally, may even be when you are very young in the Lord.

A young lady works at the telephone desk in our office in Colorado Springs. A year and a half ago she was associated with the young communist league in Great Britain. She heard Billy Graham and accepted the Lord Jesus Christ. Soon she and a couple other girls in her art and drama school were used of the Lord to win some girls to Christ. We taught Pat and some of the others, and they in turn taught the girls whom they led to Christ. Some of these have led still other girls to Christ, and they too are training their friends. Patricia is a great-grandmother already, though she is only about a year and four months old in the Lord.

We see this all the time. I know a sailor who, when he was only four months old in the Lord, was a great-grandfather. He had led some sailors to the Lord who in turn led other sailors to the Lord, and these last led still other sailors to the Lord — yet he was only four months old.

How was this done? God used the pure channel of these young Christians' lives in their exuberance and first love for Christ, and out of their hearts the incorruptible seed of the Word of God was sown in the hearts of other people. It took hold. Faith came by the hearing of the Word. They were born again by faith in the Lord Jesus Christ. They observed those Christians who led them to Christ and shared in the joy, the peace, and the thrill of it all. And in their joy, they wanted someone else to know.

In every Christian audience, I am sure there are men and women who have been Christians for five, ten, or twenty years but who do not know of one person who is living for Jesus Christ today because of them. I am not talking now about merely working for Christ, but about producing for Christ. Someone may say, "I gave out a hundred thousand tracts." That is good, but how many sheep did you bring in?

Some time ago I talked to twenty-nine missionary candidates. They were graduates of universities or Bible schools or seminaries. As a member of the board I interviewed each one over a period of five days, giving each candidate from half an hour to an hour. Among the questions I asked were two that are very important. The first one had to do with their devotional life. "How is the time you spend with the Lord? Do you feel that your devotional life is what the Lord would have it to be?"

Out of this particular group of twenty-nine only one person said, "I believe my devotional life is what it ought to be." To the others my question then was, "Why is your devotional life not what it should be?"

"Well, you see, I am here at this summer institute," was a common reply. "We have a concentrated course. We do a year's work in only ten weeks. We are so busy."

I said, "All right. Let's back up to when you were in college. Did you have victory in your devotional life then?"

"Well, not exactly."

We traced back and found that never since they came to know the Savior had they had a period of victory in their devotional lives. That was one of the reasons for their sterility — lack of communion with Christ.

The other question I asked them was, "You are going out to the foreign field. You hope to be used by the Lord in winning men and women to Christ. Is that right?"

"Yes."

"You want them to go on and live the victorious life, don't you? You don't want them just to make a decision and then go back into the world, do you?"

"No."

"Then may I ask you something more? How many persons do you know by name today who were won to Christ by you and who are living for Him?"

The majority had to admit that they were ready to cross an ocean and learn a foreign language, but they had not won their first soul who was going on with Jesus Christ. A number of them said that they got many people to go to church; others said they had persuaded some to go forward when the invitation was given.

I asked, "Are they living for Christ now?" Their eyes dropped. I then continued, "How do you expect that by crossing an ocean and speaking in a foreign language with people who are suspicious of you, whose way of life is unfamiliar, you will be able to do there what you have not done here?"

These questions do not apply to missionaries and prospective missionaries only. They apply to all of God's people. Every one of His children ought to be a reproducer.

Are you producing? If not, why not? Is it because of a lack of communion with Christ, your Lord, that closeness of fellowship that is part of the great plan? Or is it some sin in your life, an unconfessed something, that has stopped the flow? Or is it that you are still a babe? "For when for the time ye ought to be teachers, ye have need that one teach you again" (Hebrews 5:12).

How to Produce Reproducers

The reason that we are not getting this gospel to the ends of the earth is not because it is not potent enough.

Twenty-three years ago we took a born-again sailor and spent some time with him, showing him how to reproduce spiritually after his kind. It took time, lots of time. It was not a hurried, thirty-minute challenge in a church service and a hasty good-bye with an invitation to come back next week. We spent time together. We took care of his problems and taught him not only to hear God's Word and to read it, but also how to study it. We taught him how to fill the quiver of his heart with the arrows of God's Word, so that the Spirit of God could lift an arrow from his heart and place it to the bow of his lips and pierce a heart for Christ.

He found a number of boys on his ship, but none of them would go all out for the Lord. They would go to church, but when it came right down to doing something, they were "also-rans." He came to me after a month of this and said, "Dawson, I can't get any of these guys on the ship to get down to business."

I said to him, "Listen, you ask God to give you one. You can't have two until you have one. Ask God to give you a man after your own heart."

He began to pray. One day he came to me and said, "I think I've found him." Later he brought the young fellow over. Three months from the time that I started to work with him, he had found a man of like heart. This first sailor was not the kind of man you had to push and give prizes to before he would do something. He loved the Lord and was willing to pay a price to produce. He worked with this new babe in Christ, and those two fellows began to grow and spiritually reproduce. On that ship 125 men found the Savior before it was sunk at Pearl Harbor. Men off that first battleship are in four continents of the world as missionaries today. It was necessary to make a start, however. The Devil's great trick is to stop anything like this if he can before it gets started. He will stop you, too, if you let him.

There are Christians whose lives run in circles who, nevertheless, have the desire to be spiritual parents. Take a typical example. You meet him in the morning as he goes to work and say to him, "Why are you going to work?"

"Well, I have to earn money."

"What are you earning money for?" you ask.

"Well," he replies, "I have to buy food."

"What do you want food for?"

"I have to eat so as to have strength to go to work and earn some more money."

"What do you want more money for?"

"I have to buy clothes so that I can be dressed to go to work and earn some more money."

"What do you want more money for?"

"I have to buy a house or pay the rent so I will have a place to rest up, so I will be fit to work and earn some more money." And so it goes. There are many Christians like that who are going in big circles. But you continue your questioning and ask, "What else do you do?"

"Oh, I find time to serve the Lord. I am preaching here and there." But down behind all of this he has the one desire to be a spiritual father. He is praying that God will give him a man to teach. It may take six months. It need not take that long, but maybe it takes him six months to get him started taking in the Word and giving it out and getting ready to teach a man himself.

So this first man at the end of six months has another man. Each man starts teaching another in the following six months. At the end of the year, there are just four of them. Perhaps each one teaches a Bible class or helps in a street meeting, but at the same time his main interest is in his man and how he is doing. So at the end of the year the four of them get together and have a prayer meeting and determine, "Now, let's not allow anything to sidetrack us. Let's give the gospel out to a lot of people, but let's check up on at least one man and see him through."

So the four of them in the next six months each get a man. That makes eight at the end of a year and a half. They all go out after another, and at the end of two years there are sixteen men. At the end of three years there are sixty-four; the sixteen have doubled twice. At the end of five years there are 1,024. At the end of fifteen and a half years there are approximately 2,147,500,000. That is the present population of the world of persons over three years of age.

But wait a minute! Suppose that after the first man, A, helps B and B is ready to get his man while

A starts helping another, B is sidetracked, washes out, and does not produce his first man. Fifteen and a half years later you can cut your 2,147,500,000 down to 1,073,750,000 because the Devil caused B to be sterile.

God promised Abraham "in Isaac shall thy seed be called" (Genesis 21:12), so Abraham waited a long, long time for that son. God's promise to make Abraham the father of many nations was all wrapped up in that one son, Isaac. If Hitler had been present and had caused Isaac's death when Abraham had his knife poised over him on Mount Moriah, Hitler could have killed every Jew in that one stroke.

I believe that is why Satan puts all his efforts into getting the Christian busy, busy, busy, but not producing.

Men, where is your man? Women, where is your woman? Where is the one whom you led to Christ and who is now going on with Him?

There is a story in 1 Kings, chapter 20, about a man who gave a prisoner to a servant and instructed the servant to guard the prisoner well. But as the servant was busy here and there, the prisoner made his escape.

The curse of today is that we are too busy. I am not talking about being busy earning money to buy food. I am talking about being busy doing Christian things. We have spiritual activity with little productivity. And productivity comes as a result of what we call "follow-up."

Majoring in Reproducing

Five years ago Billy Graham came to me and said, "Daws, we would like you to help with our follow-up. I've been studying the great evangelists and great revivals, and I fail to see that there was much of a follow-up program. We need it. We are having an average of six thousand people come forward to decide for Christ in a month's campaign. I feel that with the work you have done you could come in and help us."

I said, "Billy, I can't follow up six thousand people. My work is always with individuals and small groups."

"Look, Daws," he answered, "everywhere I go I meet Navigators. I met them in school in Wheaton. They are in my school right now. (He was president of Northwestern Schools at that time.) There must be something to this."

"I just don't have the time," I said.

He tackled me again. The third time he pled with me and said, "Daws, I am not able to sleep nights for thinking of what happens to the converts after a crusade is over."

At that time I was on my way to Formosa (present-day Taiwan) and I said, "While I am there I will pray about it, Billy." On the sands of a Formosan beach I paced up and down two or three hours a day praying, "Lord, how can I do this? I am not even getting the work done You have given me to do. How can I take six months of the year to give to Billy?" But God laid the burden upon my heart.

Why should Billy have asked me to do it? I had said to him that day before I left for Formosa, "Billy, you will have to get somebody else."

He took me by the shoulders and said, "Who else? Who is majoring in this?" I had been majoring in it.

What will it take to jar us out of our complacency and send us home to pray, "God, give me a girl or man whom I can win to Christ, or let me take one who is already won, an infant in Christ, and try to train that one so that he or she will reproduce"?

How thrilled we are to see the masses fill up the seats! But where is your man? I would rather have an "Isaac" alive than a hundred dead, sterile, or immature.

Beginning of Follow-Up

One day years ago, I was driving along in my little Model T Ford and saw a young man walking down the street. I stopped and picked him up. As he got into the car, he swore and said, "It's sure tough to get a ride." I never hear a man take my Savior's name in vain but what my heart aches. I reached into my pocket for a tract and said, "Lad, read this."

He looked up at me and said, "Haven't I seen you somewhere before?"

I looked at him closely. He looked like someone I should know. We figured out that we had met the year before on the same road. He was on his way to a golf course to caddy when I picked him up. He had gotten into my car and had started out the same way with the name "Jesus Christ." I had taken exception to his use of that name and had opened up the New Testament and shown him the way of salvation. He had accepted Jesus Christ as his Savior. In parting I had given him Philippians 1:6, "Being confident of this very thing, that he which hath begun a good work in you will perform it until the day of Jesus Christ."

"God bless you, son. Read this," I said, and sped on my merry way.

A year later there was no more evidence of the new birth and the new creature in this boy than if he had never heard of Jesus Christ.

Winning souls was my great passion. But after I met this boy the second time on the way to the golf course, I began to go back and find some of my "converts." I want to tell you, I was sick at heart. It seemed that Philippians 1:6 was not working.

An Armenian boy came into my office one day and told me about all the souls he had won. He said that they were all Armenians, and he had the list to prove it.

I said, "Well, what is this one doing?"

He said, "That one isn't doing so good. He is backslidden."

"What about this one?" We went all down the list and there was not one living a victorious life.

I said, "Give me your Bible." I turned to Philippians and put a cardboard right under the sixth verse, took a razor blade out of my pocket, and started to come down on the page. He grabbed my hand and asked, "What are you going to do?"

"I'm going to cut this verse out," I said. "It isn't working."

Do you know what was wrong? I had been taking the sixth verse away from its context, verses 3 through 7. Paul was not just saying, "All right, the Lord has started something. He will finish it." But you know, that is what some people tell me when they win a soul. They say, "Well, I just committed him to God."

Suppose I meet someone who has a large family and say to him, "Who is taking care of your children?"

"My family? Oh, I left them with the Lord."

Right away I would say to that one, "I have a verse for you: 'But if any provide not for his own, and specially for those of his own house, he . . . is worse than an infidel'" (1 Timothy 5:8).

Paul said to the elders of the church at Ephesus, "Take heed . . . to all the flock, over the which the

Holy Ghost hath made you overseers" (Acts 20:28). You cannot make God the overseer. He makes you the overseer.

We began to work on follow-up. This emphasis on finding and helping some of the converts went on for a couple or three years before the Navigator work started. By that time our work included fewer converts but more time spent with the converts. Soon I could say, as Paul said to the Philippians, "I thank my God upon every remembrance of you, Always in every prayer of mine for you all making request with joy, For your fellowship in the gospel from the first day until now" (Philippians 1:3-5).

He followed up his converts with daily prayer and fellowship. Then he could say, "Being confident of this very thing, that he which hath begun a good work in you will perform it until the day of Jesus Christ" (Philippians 1:6). In keeping with this, the seventh verse reads: "Even as it is meet [or proper] for me to think this of you all, because I have you in my heart."

Before I had forgotten to follow up with the people God had reached through me. But from then on I began to spend the time helping them. That is why sometime later when that first sailor came to me, I saw the value of spending three months with him. I saw an Isaac in him. Isaac had Jacob, and Jacob had the twelve, and all the rest of the nation came through them.

It Takes Time to Do God's Work

You can lead a soul to Christ in twenty minutes to a couple of hours. But it takes from twenty weeks to a couple of years to get him on the road to maturity, victorious over the sins and the recurring problems that come along. He must learn how to make right decisions. He must be warned of the various "isms" that are likely to reach out with their octopus arms and pull him in and sidetrack him.

But when you get yourself a man, you have doubled your ministry—in fact, you have more than doubled your ministry. Do you know why? When you teach your man, he sees how it is done and he imitates you.

If I were the minister of a church and had deacons or elders to pass the plate and choir members to sing, I would say, "Thank God for your help. We need you. Praise the Lord for these extra things that you do," but I would keep pressing home the big job — "Be fruitful and multiply." All these other things are incidental to the supreme task of winning a man or woman to Jesus Christ and then helping him or her to go on.

Where is your man? Where is your woman? Do you have one? You can ask God for one. Search your hearts. Ask the Lord, "Am I spiritually sterile? If I am, why am I?"

Don't let your lack of knowledge stand in the way. It used to be the plan of The Navigators in the early days that whenever the sailors were with us for supper each fellow was asked at the end of the meal to quote a verse.

I would say it this way, "Quote a verse you have learned in the past forty-eight hours if you have one. Otherwise, just give us a verse." One evening as we quoted verses around the table, my little three-year-old daughter's turn came. There was a new sailor next to her who did not think about her quoting Scripture, so without giving her an opportunity, he began. She looked up at him as much as to say, "I am a human being," then she quoted John 3:16 in her own way. "For God so loved the world, dat he gave his only forgotten son, dat *whosoever* believeth in him should not perish, but have everlasting life." She put the emphasis on the "whosoever" because when she was first taught the verse she could not pronounce that word.

Days later that sailor came over and said to me, "You know, I was going to quote that verse of Scripture. It was the only one I knew. But I didn't really know it, not until little Ruthie quoted it. When she said 'whosoever,' I thought, 'that means me.' Back on the ship I accepted the Lord." Today that young man is a missionary in South America.

Until several years after we were married, my wife's father did not know the Lord. Here again God used children to reach a hungry heart. When Ruthie was three and Bruce was five, they went to visit Grandpa and Grandma. Grandpa tried to get them to repeat nursery rhymes. He said "Mary Had a Little Lamb" and "Little Boy Blue," but the children just looked at him and asked, "Who is Little Boy Blue?" He thought they did not know very much.

Their mother said, "They know some things. Quote Romans 3:23, Bruce." Bruce did. Then he asked, "Shall I quote another one, Grandpa?"

"Sure," said Grandpa.

Bruce began to quote verses of Scripture, some fifteen in all, and Ruth quoted some in between. This delighted Grandpa. He took them over to the neighbors and to the aunts and uncles, showing them how well these children knew the Scriptures. In the meantime the Word of God was doing its work. It was not long before the Holy Spirit, through the voices of babes, planted the seed in his heart. "Out of the mouth of babes and sucklings hast thou ordained strength" (Psalm 8:2).

Soul-winners are not soul-winners because of what they know, but because of the Person they know, how well they know Him, and how much they long for others to know Him.

"Oh, but I am afraid," someone says. Remember, "The fear of man bringeth a snare: but whoso putteth his trust in the LORD shall be safe" (Proverbs 29:25). Nothing under heaven except sin, immaturity, and lack of communion will put you in a position in which you cannot reproduce. Furthermore, there is not anything under heaven that can keep a newly born-again one from going on with the Lord if he has a spiritual parent to take care of him and give him the spiritual food God has provided for his normal growth.

Effects obey their causes by irresistible laws. When you sow the seed of God's Word you will get results. Not every heart will receive the Word, but some will and the new birth will take place. When a soul is born, give it the care that Paul gave new believers. Paul believed in follow-up work. He was a busy evangelist, but he took time for follow-up. The New Testament is largely made up of Paul's letters, which were follow-up letters to the converts.

James believed in it. "But be ye doers of the word, and not hearers only," he said in James 1:22. Peter believed in it. "As newborn babes, desire the sincere milk of the word, that ye may grow thereby" (1 Peter 2:2). John believed in it. "I have no greater joy than to hear that my children walk in truth" (3 John 4). All the writings of Peter, Paul, James, and most of John's are food for the new Christian.

The gospel spread to the known world during the first century without radio, television, or the printing press because these produced men who were reproducing. But today we have a lot of "pew-sitters"—people think that if they are faithful in church attendance, put good-sized gifts into the offering plate, and get people to come, they have done their part.

Where is your man? Where is your woman? Where is your boy? Where is your girl? Every one of us, no matter what age we are, should get busy memorizing Scripture. In one Sunday school class a woman seventy-two years of age and another who was seventy-eight finished The Navigators Topical Memory System. They then had something to give.

Load your heart with this precious Seed. You will find that God will direct you to those whom you can lead to Christ. There are many hearts ready for the gospel now.